Narcissism Problem Solution:

What to Do if Your Partner, Parent, Friend or Work Colleague is a Narcissist?

By

Eva Delano

Table of Contents

Introduction 5

Chapter 1. Etymology 6

Chapter 2. Narcissism and Egocentrism 7

Chapter 3. Healthy vs. Extreme 8

Chapter 4. How it Occurs 10

Chapter 5. Can it Be Reversed? 15

Chapter 6. What You Can Do 18

Chapter 7. If You Are a Friend/Partner 24

Chapter 8. If You Are a Colleague 27

Chapter 9. If You Are a Family Member 29

Conclusion 31

Thank You Page 32

Narcissism Problem Solution: What to Do if Your Partner, Parent, Friend or Work Colleague is a Narcissist?

By Eva Delano

© Copyright 2014 Eva Delano

Reproduction or translation of any part of this work beyond that permitted by section 107 or 108 of the 1976 United States Copyright Act without permission of the copyright owner is unlawful. Requests for permission or further information should be addressed to the author.

This publication is designed to provide accurate and authoritative information in regard to the subject matter covered. This work is sold with the understanding that the publisher is not engaged in rendering legal, accounting, or other professional services. If legal advice or other expert assistance is required, the services of a competent professional person should be sought.

First Published, 2014

Printed in the United States of America

Introduction

Have you noticed anyone from your workplace who seems to not care of the feelings of the people around him or her, but seems to be ironically socially skillful? Are you suffering from a certain degree of depression because the person you are with displays absurd behaviors? Are you getting tired putting up with your friend's daily exaggerations of self-worth? Are you frustrated with your job because your boss just threatened to fire you because you are accused of challenging him? If you have experienced any of these, you might be in the presence of a narcissist. To validate, read on.

Understanding narcissism could be both frustrating and exciting, as knowing more about it can give you mixed feelings, depending on which perspective you decide to take. However, in order to overcome the possibility of frustration, learn that there are things you can do in case you have around you at work, or at home, a narcissist person. You will get to know how the term was coined, its difference from egocentrism, its levels, and what can be done about it.

Chapter 1. Etymology

The term, Narcissism, can be traced back the young hunter named Narcissus, who is known in Greek mythology to be remarkably conceited, that he scorned those who loved him. The highlight of his story revolves around how he fell in love with his own reflection, which he saw in the pool, and died like that. In one version, among several others, he had no knowledge that it was himself he was falling for, and as he was so into the image he encounter by the pool of water, he could not leave 'it', and so he drowned. In another version, Narcissus committed suicide upon the realization that he will never be able to get the object of his love – himself.

In either version, Narcissus is depicted as a self-fixated man, who cared about nobody but himself. For this reason, along with others, the state of being self-absorbed and apathetic, if not hateful of others, is called Narcissism, or having the qualities of Narcissus, the arrogant, self-loving character.

Chapter 2. Narcissism and Egocentrism

Narcissism is usually mistaken as a synonym to egocentrism, indeed they have large similarities. However, they are still two different things. Narcissism is a basically fixation with oneself. Egocentrism refers to the state of having a failure to differentiate between self and other, and is part and parcel of narcissism. What an egocentric person and a narcissist share in common is the belief that they are the center of attention. What an egocentric person does not necessarily have that a narcissist has is the sense of gratification by one's own admiration.

This being said, it is safe to conclude that egocentrism is one of the manifestations of a narcissistic condition, which may vary according to gravity. There are persons who manifest narcissistic traits but do not necessarily qualify to have the disorder. Some persons fall under those who are extreme narcissists, while others qualify as what is specifically considered as healthy narcissist.

Chapter 3. Healthy vs. Extreme

Yes you read it right. There are certain degrees in which narcissistic manifestations can be 'healthy' or relatively 'normal' in a person bearing them. While extreme narcissism is much easier to detect, normal narcissists have just 'some' amount of 'basic' narcissism , which render them just responsibly looking after themselves.

The very egotistical preoccupation of an extreme narcissist can be found in his or her personal inclinations, ambitions, desires, and achievements, among so many other attributes of the self – the same thing a normal narcissist may be concerned about, but not at a disturbing extent – both to the self and to others.

The extreme narcissists are particularly engrossed with others perceive them. It freaks them out to sense that they do not look good to other people, and thus makes them leave a relationship when the other party makes them look 'bad'. They tend to become emotionally isolated as they could cut others off when they perceive that staying with them threatens the personal image/s they are trying to project.

Chapter 4. How it Occurs

The extreme narcissist's tendency to look at people as objects generally comes from that he or she is totally absorbed in his or her self. In the perspective of psychologists, this characteristic of a narcissist is something developed, and is far from being genetic, and roots back to a period in his or her life, when he or she was significantly wounded emotionally, eventually getting traumatizing with an encounter with detachment. This explains a major attachment dysfunction that is rather internal, as the narcissist can be observed to manage to have excellent social skills to mask the dysfunction – intentionally or otherwise.

This emotional trauma experienced by the extreme narcissist is usually an unresolved childhood conflict, from which he or she has not moved on. It is said that the extreme narcissist is frozen in childhood, that specific period where he or she was subjected to the devastatingly traumatic experience. This explains why narcissists usually have a much younger emotional age and maturity. Emotionally, they stop growing at the stage they got stuck. They could not level up because there are unresolved issues.

Aside from retaining the same emotional age and maturity from the time of the trauma, the extreme narcissist is also said to have created a certain shield as a means for emotional survival. In the emotional trauma he or she had experienced in childhood, which most likely resulted to a notion that he or she could not trust anybody, since no appropriate or healthy option for him or her was apparent to have the conflict fixed in a healthy manner, the extreme narcissist had to develop defense mechanisms that he could utilize to be able to make end meet, so to speak.

Most of the time, the protective barrier that the narcissist almost permanently brings with him or her is a false persona. In much more lay term, a mask.

A personality disorder

The established persistent pattern of behaving and relating to self, to others and to the environment called personality. It is said to include perceptions, attitudes and emotions. Sometimes, personality is used interchangeable with behavior, or attitude. But these they have similarities, but behavior and attitude are just two aspects of your personality. Your personality is something that has been affected by abroad array of situations, knowledge, and experiences over time, and thus cannot be easily altered. While your personality is largely affected by what and whom you deal with, such as the environment and other people, it is also closely linked to biologic and genetic makeup.

Disorder comes in when your personality becomes unyielding and maladaptive, and most importantly, when your personality already causes you distress, and interferes significantly with how you function socially. A diagnosis of a personality disorder is made by the doctor when you start displaying enduing behavioral patterns that deviate from social norms in at least a couple of the following: cognition, affect, interpersonal functioning, and impulse control. Cognition comprises of how you view or take yourself, others, and the environment, while emotional response includes the strength, range, lability, and pertinence. Moreover, impulse control is your capability to take control of your compulsions, or impulse, or convey certain conduct with reverence to the proper timing and venue.

A narcissistic personality is characterized by 1) a ubiquitous pattern of grandiosity, whether in fantasy or in behavior, 2) a need for veneration, and 3) shortage of empathy. Psychiatric standards can help you distinguish between a person to have narcissistic personality disorder and one who merely has narcissistic traits. Similar with 'healthy' narcissists, people with narcissistic traits may have a certain level of these characteristics, but to not go as far as becoming inflexible, poor in adaptation, emotionally distressed, or socially dysfunctional.

Having a pervasive pattern of grandiose affectation, persons with this personality disorder may either blatantly express their grandiosity, or choose to discreetly presume to be acknowledged for their perceived achievements. Their fantasies which they have preoccupations of may be boundless success, authority, virtuosity, or magnificence, among others. This is where the reinforcement of their sense of superiority comes from. The usually silently mull over privilege and entitlement; they also think of themselves as better than privileged personalities.

Since these persons are in dire need of constant attention and admiration, they quickly take offense from criticism. As such, although not instantly noticed due to their exceptional outward social skills, their self-esteem is nearly always delicate and weak. Moreover, their arrogance can be seen in their consistent display of sense of entitlement, marked by an absurd anticipation of instant fulfillment of their wants, or of very special treatment. Failure of another to satisfy this person's expectations leaves them either confused, or furious.

Chapter 5. Can it Be Reversed?

Narcissism as a personality disorder is longstanding, as personality characteristics, as mentioned earlier, cannot be easily altered. This partly explains why the person who may have it still behave the same way no matter how distressing it is for them. While there is no medication to 'cure' or alter the personality, therapy, although expected to act in a very slow manner and in a long term fashion, can be designed. This is not going to be very easy, especially for people who do not recognize their own problem as a source of difficulty. For people who believe that problems arising from their conditions are caused by things, circumstances, or people other than their own selves, treatment is rather difficult, and may be even frustrating for their health care providers. If this is the case with professionals as they are, you may expect that this can be hard for you too, whether you are a family member, a friend or a significant other.

The primary step to dealing with a person with a narcissistic personality disorder, for both professionals and concerned loved ones is to have a good set of self-awareness skills. Having such is very important because it will allow overcoming general difficulties taking care of narcissistic persons. It is also helpful in your need to refuse to internalize criticisms, arrogance, impatience and harsh actions that may be encountered along the way.

In the treatment of narcissistic personality disorder, it is crucial to seek safe and competent assistance from an expert who is adept in 'healing' trauma. Although there is a wide array of options for counselors who are licensed and have more than the minimum requirements to do their job, choosing somebody who can competently deal with such delicate case is critical. In doing so, it is vital to keep in mind that narcissists have major trust issues, which are rooted from an experience they have been guarding almost all their life.

Next, the person with narcissistic personality disorder should have a good preparation, in order for him or her to become willing to 'feel' again. Since he or she has long mastered to live and function under the shield to detachment, which he has built as a means to survive a perceived world that attacks and wounds, this could be a very difficult struggle to go through. However, this is a very important move in salvaging left-behind emotional age and maturity, given some effective professional intervention to hurdle this, your loved one is on his or her way to getting better.

While doctors and nurses take care about the medical, professional and technical aspects of this psychiatric condition, your role as a sibling, parent, child, friend, companion, husband or wife to the 'patient' is very crucial.

Chapter 6. What You Can Do

Whether you are a parent, a sibling, a child, a friend, a colleague or a partner of a person with narcissism, there is always something you can do to help him or her. Generally, if you intend to play a more therapeutic role to your loved one who has a personality disorder, you can be guided by three things.

1. You yourself should be self-aware, and free from extra baggages. Having someone else you can discuss your own feelings of frustration will help you deal better with your loved one, who needs much more sensitive emotional responses from you. Keep them effective.

2. Now having a clearer understanding of what your loved one is going through, you should be more aware of the manifestations he or she has of the problem. Since you can better see through the person, expect to recognize some attempts of manipulation, and be ready to deal with them. It will help if you exert some efforts to be firm and consistent.

3. Expect too, that your loved one may view you as in control of him or her, and of the relationship. This may lead to his view of you as threatening, so take necessary action to manage it. That is, if you are decided to indeed take such role.

Support. Basically, is it providing support that you can do to help, as part of the person's support system. It may appear too simple, trivial, and probably even easy, but right now, you may want to think again. Providing support entails commitment – emotionally and physically. Sounds fun? Keep reading.

Emotional commitment could be one of the most difficult things you can promise anyone. You have a life of your own, baggages to carry, and other people to care for. However, committing yourself to support a loved one in his or her personality struggles is not exactly an emotional obligation, but simply a commitment that may influence you emotionally, if you do not handle it well. Good news is there are tips on how to secure your emotional side while dealing with rather difficult personalities.

Also, providing support could be physically exhausting, especially when you have become more aware that the actuations of the person you are looking after are socially unacceptable, unfair and uncalled for. It can push you to your limits emotionally, and in turn, physically, as your body manifests what your emotions are feeling. When you emotionally feel bad, your body reacts. So, one way to avoid physical stress is to guard your emotions.

Be self-aware. It has been mentioned ahead that becoming self-aware, as well as maintaining self-awareness skills, is key, whether you are a medical professional or a member of the support system. This is very important because it is only when you have established a keen sense of self-awareness that you are capable to be aware of the environment, and of others – that is, the narcissist in your family, at work, or in your social circle. (This is one of the difficulties with narcissists, as they sometimes fail to see their problem. They therefore cannot feel for others.)

Ensure trustworthiness. You are now aware that the person with a narcissistic personality disorder is severely distrustful, that even counselors and doctors may have a hard time gaining his or her confidence. You, on the other hand, being part of his or her support system, have, in one way or another, earned a certain level of trust. Do not ruin it. In fact, if your presence in this stage of his or her struggle will only take away the existing trusting relationship you have with the person, better leave the job to somebody who will be more helpful. You can always extend your support from a distance.

Empathize. More than becoming aware of others, however, is being able to empathize, that is essential in supporting your narcissist loved one. Coupled with your ability to put yourself in the shoes of this person, is knowing what to expect is wearing them. Keeping in mind that you are in a better position than this person, to understand his or her situation, realize that as he or she goes on with whatever design of therapy he is enrolled in, he or she is not exactly having the best time. In the process of empathizing, or as it is usually described, putting your feet in their shoes, you are allowing yourself to understand as exactly as possible, what he is going through. Consider for instance how your loved one should be able to get to the point of willingness to go back to his or her past feelings.

Imagine yourself getting severely threatened, without any perceived help around. You are on your own. You have no one to count on but yourself. You can either die of the pain, or endure it while finding a way to make the pain less excruciating. Little by little, you learn to benumb yourself. Over time, you made it to the rather superficial goal you used to be so desperate about. Finally, you are free from pain. You are in control, and nobody can touch that part ever again.

And now you are being told to take the shield off, let go, go back to that time of terror and feel the agony all over. What do you feel? Are you reluctant? Are you angry? Do you feel invaded?

In this manner of empathizing, you get to know profoundly how deep the pain can be, and also get to answer questions that may explain more episodes of your loved one's difficult behavior. In empathizing however, you get to protect yourself from being emotionally affected, as in sympathizing. Empathizing is considered the therapeutic version of sympathy, because while you exhibit concern for another, you do not cry with him or her, not bring along with you the burden. It is by empathizing that you can more effectively be functional in supporting your loved one in the struggles that he or she may be going through.

Chapter 7. If You Are a Friend/Partner

Especially if you are a spouse, your tendency in dealing with a person with the disorder is to sacrifice part of yourself in order for your partner to live his or her grandiosity-filled, non-empathic life, as it may be tiring for you avoid relational conflicts so you just decide to give up and give in, leaving you miserable around him or her, and relieved in his or her absence. This is not healthy for you. And if you think you are doing your partner a favor, guess what: you are not. In providing your friend or partner rather genuine help, and in being fair with yourself too, there are things that you can do in your capacity of being his or her other.

Check on his/her awareness and willingness. As said, it is most difficult to treat people with the disorder when they themselves are in denial of the source of their problems. In helping your loved one here, it is as difficult when they do not have a sense of recognition of their problem. This could be a defense mechanism your loved one is exhibiting. Denial hinders your loved one to admit that something is wrong. In case you can, it will be very helpful for him or her, and also for the attending professionals, if you can assist him or her to such realization. Again, doing so takes knowledge, skills and credibility. So, be careful.

Being part of the prerequisites to treatment, your loved one's willingness to change is preceded by his or her admission that something is wrong. In case the latter has been achieved, then know if he or she wants to keep going. As he or she decides on this, pressure is the least you should give. Instead, provide a rather supportive atmosphere, one that keeps his or her humanity intact, one that is nonjudgmental, one that is helpful.

Be careful of your own behavior. Again, this is preceded by a great deal of self-awareness. If you are trying to support someone who has problems with behavior, then yours should also be strategically displayed. This means that you cannot afford to be careless with how you behave, as you could be a source of strength of the person you are trying to support. If you grow impatient with how the person thinks or acts, then this will only create further problems. You are not fit to be among the members of his or her support system, as you are not able to comply with implications of the primary requirement on self-awareness.

Chapter 8. If You Are a Colleague

The things you can do for your narcissistic co-worker are similar with the things a friend can do. In addition, you may also consider what follow.

Maintain distance. Some emotional distance between you and the narcissist is especially healthy in the workplace. While you are not really expected to be socially intimate with a colleague, you are also expected to communicate with them. This does not mean, however, that you should avoid the person. You are merely setting limits on your distance, which also helps reduce, if not avoid, incidents of arguing, which will only lead to the person's possible feelings of depression or anger, and your feeling of frustration.

Avoid unnecessary confrontations. Know that your narcissist colleague is not an ordinary co-worker. Especially if he or she is your boss, challenging him or her directly can cause problems both on your working relationship, and your job. It is important that you convey your support and appreciation to the person. However, if the need for a confrontation is inevitable, consider speaking with his or her superior, if approaching him in a group to express your concern tactfully is not feasible. This may sound relatively unethical, but working under the supervision of a narcissist boss is one special case.

Chapter 9. If You Are a Family Member

Aside from what are already written above, if a member of your family has narcissistic personality disorder, or simply narcissism, know that family therapy is an option in helping out. However, since the painful experiences the person has tried to overcome, mask and forget usually originate from family relations, it could be tormenting for the person to go through it.

Nonetheless, given the expertise of a well-chosen therapist, the ultimate purpose of a family therapy should not be defeated. As you carefully engage in a family therapy, know that you are doing this to help the person become more aware of his wounded feelings, which led him or her to deal with people in an arrogant and superior manner, which is also possibly painful for the other party. While in therapy, the same principles of self-awareness and empathy are applied, in order for you to be able to show support.

Remember, however, that because the fact that family experiences may be too painful to recall is a crucial factor present in this option, it important that a narcissist only engage in family (or group) counseling once he or she had progressed well in individual counseling. Such should only be done as well, in the presence of an effective therapist – one who not only has the educational credentials and related experience, but of equal importance, has the passion and sincerity to help improve the quality of the life not only of the narcissist family member, but also the entire family he or she belongs to.

Conclusion

All in all, knowing that a narcissist thinks he is omnipotent, superior and invulnerable, will help you in numerous ways as you try to cope with one, be it at home, at work, or within your social circles. More than seeing the narcissist person as an arrogant crazy being, you now have the opportunity to look at your partner, your family member, or your colleague, beyond the mask that he or she so painstakingly created, in order to shield him or herself from more pain that may be inflicted towards him or her. You, at some point may be one of those he or she may perceive as an attacker, based on how you sometimes respond during certain circumstances. But now that you have the knowledge, you know better.

This is your chance to be a better partner, parent, sibling, colleague or friend. The person behind the narcissistic characteristics needs you. He or she may not know it yet, or maybe he or she does. You wouldn't know for sure. But you now know you can help.

Thank You Page

I want to personally thank you for reading my book. I hope you found information in this book useful and I would be very grateful if you could leave your honest review about this book. I certainly want to thank you in advance for doing this.

If you have the time, you can check my other books too.

www.ingramcontent.com/pod-product-compliance
Lightning Source LLC
LaVergne TN
LVHW021745060526
838200LV00052B/3486